The Church History Catechism

The German Reformation

The purpose of this work is to operate as a means of instruction, encouragement, and edification to the saints of God in this generation and, Lord willing, that which is to come, until Christ returns.
Amen.

Soli Deo Gloria

by C. Stewart

authorHOUSE®

AuthorHouse™
1663 Liberty Drive
Bloomington, IN 47403
www.authorhouse.com
Phone: 1-800-839-8640

© 2011 C. Stewart. All Rights Reserved

No part of this book may be reproduced, stored in
a retrieval system, or transmitted by any means
without the written permission of the author.

First published by AuthorHouse 01/21/2011

ISBN: 978-1-4520-2821-7 (sc)
ISBN: 978-1-4520-2822-4 (e)

Library of Congress Control Number: 2011900326

Printed in the United States of America

Any people depicted in stock imagery provided by Thinkstock are models,
and such images are being used for illustrative purposes only.
Certain stock imagery © Thinkstock.

This book is printed on acid-free paper.

Because of the dynamic nature of the Internet, any Web addresses or
links contained in this book may have changed since publication and
may no longer be valid. The views expressed in this work are solely those
of the author and do not necessarily reflect the views of the publisher,
and the publisher hereby disclaims any responsibility for them.

I would like to thank my wife, Summer, for encouraging me to continue with this work and have it prepared for the saints at Grace Gospel Church. I would also like to thank them for their desire and passion for the history of the Church, especially to the youth of the Church who were the ones engaged in the extensive use of this catechism.

Introduction

In your hands you hold a historical catechism which was developed to give Christians an understanding of the German Reformation. Catechetical instruction has been a popular and effective form for the instruction of children and adults alike throughout the history of the Church. I am pleased, therefore, that I have had an opportunity to produce this small work and I pray that it would be used to help bring an understanding of Church History to the minds of Christians. I, furthermore, pray that the Lord would be pleased to grant that I will be able to produce other such works—those detailing other periods throughout the history of the Church—in the future for the edification and instruction of the saints.

I would like to mention at the outset that the statements and answers presented in this Catechism are historical facts to the best of my knowledge through the research I have done. Some may disagree with the beliefs and actions of the historical characters that are presented here, but that does not change the fact that the events and beliefs presented herein is how the history in this time-period unfolded. I just pray that this work would be useful for all who use it; that many would learn from these heroic figures who managed to turn the world upside down by the rediscovery of the Gospel in the 16th century.

In looking at the history of the Christian Church we need to stress that it is indeed a critical field of study. For this reason I felt that it was fitting to produce this historical catechism which deals with a specific historical time-frame of the Church. When we study Church history there are some points that need to be considered.

Firstly, we need to ask ourselves the question: What is Church history? Church history might best be considered as two rails of a track, upon which the actual Church (considered as the people of God) continues to travel through time. These two rails consist of "progressive revelation" and "historical theology".

Progressive revelation is that process whereby God has been pleased to reveal Himself to the world. This revelation was given through God's people and has been preserved in written form. This written revelation is referred to as the Bible; the infallible, inerrant Word of God which was written over a 1500 year period of time, by above 40 men who were "moved along" by the Holy Spirit to write only that which is the truth (2 Pet. 1:21). In their writings they wrote with their own faculties and personalities, yet they only penned that which God decreed should be put down.

Historical theology, on the other hand, could be broadly define as the response of God's people to progressive revelation. In other words, as God people study and understand the Word more fully they gain a deeper understanding, over time, of His redemptive purposes. This was seen on a grand scale during the time of the Reformation when the Reformers *rediscovered* and further *developed* and *systematized* the truths taught since the earliest days of the Church.

If I were to illustrate this point I would direct you to consider a pair of binoculars or a telescope. As you behold an object in the distance through the binoculars or telescope it may at first appear small and undefined. As the dial is turned, however, the image becomes more clear; definition is seen in the object yet the image is not altered or different in anyway then when you first looked. The only difference is that you are now able to make out specific detail in the object. In like fashion, progressive revelation, strictly speaking, ended with the closing of the canon of Scripture in 397 AD at the council of Carthage. However, what might be called a "secondary revelation" or "further illumination" continues beyond the time of the closing of the canon of Scripture, until the time of Christ's return. This process includes the discovery of a *clearer interpretation* and *application* of Scripture, as well as the events which lead to those discoveries. It also includes the effect that these discoveries have on the history of God's people, as well as the harmful effects of false doctrine upon the people of God. This continuing process is outlined at Ephesians 4:8-16 which says, *"Wherefore he saith, When he ascended up on high, he led captivity captive, and gave gifts unto men.(Now that he ascended, what is it but that he also descended first into the lower parts of the earth? He that descended is the same also that ascended up far above all heavens, that he might fill all things.) And he gave some, apostles; and some, prophets; and some, evangelists; and some, pastors and teachers; For the perfecting of the saints, for the work of the ministry, for the edifying of the body of Christ: Till we all come in the unity of the faith, and of the knowledge of the Son of God, unto a perfect man, unto the measure of the stature of the fulness of Christ: That we [henceforth] be no more children, tossed t and fro, and carried about with every wind of doctrine, by the sleight of men, [and] cunning craftiness, whereby they lie in wait to deceive; But speaking the truth in love, may grow up into him in all things, which is the head, [even] Christ: From whom the whole body fitly joined together and compacted by that which every joint supplieth, according to the effectual working in the measure of every part, maketh increase of the body unto the edifying of itself in love."* This "secondary revelation" or "further illumination" is called historical theology. Together with progressive revelation they constitute Church history.

Secondly, I need to put forth the ever relevant question: Why study Church history? The simple answer to this question is so that we might avoid the mistakes of the past (Rom. 15:4; 1 Cor. 10:1-12). Proverbs 22:28 says, *"Remove not the ancient landmark, which thy fathers have set."* Though directed primarily against transgression of land ownership, I am not in violation to make spiritual application from this verse. Church history reveals those "landmarks" of *doctrine* and *practice* that God has been pleased to reveal to us, via His word. Church history further reveals the blessings that come by heeding those landmarks, as well as the cursing that comes from disobeying the same (Dt. 11).

Furthermore, we are to study Church history to maintain a godly flexibility as we face the present and consider the future. The Christian reality is not static. Rather, God's redemptive purposes revealed to the world through His Church continues throughout time looking for the return of the Lord. In this, challenges will arise from the godless culture of the world outside the Church (1 Jn. 2:15-17; Jas. 4:4) and from inside the Church, due to the presence of false teachers within church ranks (Jude 4; 2 Pet. 2:1-3; Acts 20:28-30).To maintain the survival of the Church (Mt. 16:18), the Church returns to Scripture as its primary resource for that survival. The Spirit, however, also brings to the mind of the Church those things which have gone before. In these things that have come before, the Church can detect old errors in new dress, and can also find older, but ever potent, weapons for her defense.

In this way the Church can ever meet the challenges of the current day, and can smile at the future.

Lastly, and speaking specifically about this catechism, I need to ask: How are we to use this Historical Catechism? The burden I have had in the production of this catechism is that the people of God in this generation, and that which is to come (if the Lord tarries), would gain insight and edification from the events and circumstances that the saints of God found themselves facing in previous generations. The proper use of this catechism, therefore, is of prime importance.

I, therefore, recommend that each question be viewed as an opportunity to wed Historical events with Biblical theology. By saying this, I mean that the events which have happened in the history of the Church *must* be used to convey Biblical theology as we view the experience of those in past ages. Events which have happened to the saints of God in the past are an excellent field for us to learn about the nature of God, His dealing with man (both His Church and those who oppose her), the power of the Gospel, and various other theological subjects handled throughout the progress of time. For this reason, I would encourage teachers and students alike that they not only think "historically" but also "theologically" in the use of this catechism.

I also recommend, if possible, that full consideration be given to each question; that is, that you take your time in the study of Church history. This is obviously based on the setting in which you are using this catechism. For example, if you are using it (as I have for many years) during your devotional time with younger children, then memorizing the contents will more then suffice. As they get older, however, there will be an opportunity to take your time and enter into a more full historical/theological discussion with them. The same is true with an adult study. In the discussion I advise that the teacher would expound both the historical relevance and theological realities of the event under scrutiny. The questions and answers in this catechism have been designed to act merely as a "skeleton" so that the students would be able to grasp a framework of the history being discussed, which will also allow the teacher the liberty to add "meat" to the lesson.

I pray in the name of our Lord and Savior Jesus Christ that this work would be a blessing to you and all those who make up the body of Christ (the Church) in this generation and that which is to come if the Lord tarries. May the Lord grant you with a full measure and understanding of His working through men, in time, for eternity.

C. Stewart
   with
James Parker, a dear brother, friend, and teacher in Christ

Q. 1. What was the Reformation?

A. The Reformation was the providential move of God whereby He revived the Christian religion.

Q. 2. What are the three fundamental principles of the Reformation?

A. The three fundamental principles of the Reformation are: the authority of the Scriptures over tradition, the primacy of faith over works, and the Priesthood of all believers over the Roman Catholic Priesthood.

Q. 3. What are the 'Five Sola's' of the Reformation?

A. The 'Five Sola's' of the Reformation are: Sola Fide (Faith Alone), Sola Christus (Christ Alone), Sola Gratia (Grace Alone), Sola Scriptura (Scripture Alone), and Soli Deo Gloria (God's Glory Alone).

Q. 4. Who did God use to ignite the Reformation in Germany?

A. God used Martin Luther, a monk of the Augustinian order, to ignite the Reformation in Germany.

Q. 5. Who was Luther's spiritual father before the Reformation broke forth?

A. Luther's spiritual father was John Von Staupitz, who, as Luther said, *"first caused the light of the gospel to shine in the darkness of my heart."*

Q. 6. At which university was Luther the professor of theology?

A. Luther was the professor of theology at Wittenburg, Germany.

Q. 7. Which verse of Scripture deeply convicted Luther that man could only be righteous by faith alone in Jesus Christ alone?

A. The verse of Scripture which deeply convicted Luther was Romans 1:17, *"For therein is the righteousness of God revealed from faith to faith: as it is written, The just shall live by faith."*

Q. 8. When did the Reformation begin?

A. The Reformation began on October 31, 1517.

Q. 9. What did Luther write that started the Reformation?

A. Luther wrote his '95 Theses' (also titled: 'Disputation to explain the Virtue of Indulgences').

Q. 10. Why did Luther write the 95 Theses?

A. Luther wrote the 95 Theses to protest the abuse of the selling of 'Indulgences'.

Q. 11. What is an Indulgence?

A. An Indulgence is an unbiblical Roman Catholic practice of paying money to the Church in order to decrease the amount of time one spends in Purgatory.

Q. 12. What is Purgatory?

A. Purgatory is the unscriptural doctrine held by the Roman Catholic and Greek Orthodox churches, that all who die at peace with the church, but are not yet perfect, must undergo purifying suffering for sin.

Q. 13. Who was commissioned to sell indulgences near the section of Germany where Luther lived?

A. The man commissioned to sell indulgences near where Luther lived was a Dominican monk named John Tetzel, who was prior of a convent, doctor of philosophy, and papal inquisitor.

Q. 14. What was the famous saying of Tetzel which is remembered to this day?

A. The famous saying of Teztel is: "*When the coin in the coffer rings, a soul from Purgatory springs.*"

Q. 15. Who commissioned Tetzel to sell Indulgences in Germany?

A. Albrecht, Archbishop of Mainz, commissioned Tetzel to sell Indulgences in Germany.

Q. 16. Why did Albrecht commission Tetzel to sell Indulgences?

A. Albrecht commissioned Tetzel because the Pope needed money to rebuild St. Peter's Church in Rome.

Q. 17. How were the 95 Theses circulated so quickly, both to the common man as well as to the educated scholar?

A. The 95 Theses were circulated so quickly by being translated from Latin into German, and then printed en masse and carried from house to house by colportors, students, and friends.

Q. 18. Where and when did Luther, for the first time, defend the doctrines of natural depravity, the bondage of the will, regenerating grace, faith, and good works?

A. Luther first defended these doctrines in April, 1518, in a public debate at Heidelberg.

Q. 19. What good came from the debate at Heidelberg?

A. The good that came from the Heidelberg debate was that Luther found considerable response and sowed more of the seed of the Reformation.

Q. 20. When Luther was cited to appear in Rome to recant of his "heresies", did he go?

A. No. Elector Frederick the Wise, unwilling to sacrifice Luther to the Roman inquisition, arranged a peaceful interview with Cardinal Cajetan at the Diet of Augsburg.

Q. 21. What was the result of the Diet of Augsburg?

A. The result of the Diet of Augsburg was that Luther met with Cajetan three times and refused to recant.

Q. 22. Where and when did Luther publicly debate the subject of the papacy?

A. Luther publicly debated the subject of the papacy at the Leipzig Disputation in 1519.

Q. 23. Who did Luther debate at this disputation?

A. Luther debated at this disputation Dr. John Eck, a defender of Romanism and the papacy.

Q. 24. What was the difference in argument between Eck and Luther?

A. The difference in argument between Eck and Luther was that Eck maintained that the Pope is the successor to Peter, and the Vicar of Christ by divine right; Luther, however, knew this claim to be contrary to Scripture, to the ancient church, and to the council of Nicea.

Q. 25. What evidence did each use to defend their case?

A. Eck primarily produced evidence from selective church tradition and decrees of past Popes to defend his case, while Luther primarily produced evidence from the Word of God.

Q. 26. What was the result of the Leipzig disputation?

A. The result of the Leipzig disputation was that Luther made a deep impression upon many younger men who departed from the university at Leipzig and came to Wittenburg.

Q. 27. Shortly after this disputation, what conviction did Luther and others come to?

A. After the Leipzig disputation Luther and others came to the conviction that the Pope was the Anti-Christ, and that the Roman Catholic system was the very stronghold of Satan.

Q. 28. What three Reformation treatises did Luther write in rapid succession after coming to this conclusion?

A. Luther wrote, in rapid succession: the 'Address to the German Nobility', the 'Babylonian Captivity of the Church', and the 'Freedom of a Christian Man'.

Q. 29. What were these books about?

A. The first two were a trumpet, calling men to war against the Roman system, while the last is a beautiful work detailing the Christian life.

Q. 30. What did the Pope, and the Roman Catholic Church, do in reaction to Luther's protest?

A. In reaction to Luther's protest, the Roman Catholic Church excommunicated Martin Luther by issuing a Papal Bull, which was sent to him on June 15th 1520.

Q. 31. What is a Papal Bull?

A. A Papal Bull is an official letter or edict from the Pope. It comes from the Latin word *bulla* which means "a seal".

Q. 32. Why was this Bull historically significant?

A. This Bull was historically significant because it was the last Bull addressed to the Western Church as a whole, and the first one which was disobeyed by a major portion of it.

Q. 33. Who was the Pope that excommunicated Martin Luther?

A. The Pope that excommunicated Martin Luther was Leo X.

Q. 34. What did Luther do with this Papal Bull?

A. Luther burned this Papal Bull.

Q. 35. What else did Luther burn along with the Bull?

A. Luther burned, along with this Bull, the papal decretals, the code of canon law, and several writings of Eck and Emser who were Roman Catholic theologians.

Q. 36. What was the response of the Roman Catholic Church to Luther's protest at this time?

A. In response to Luther's protest at this time, the Pope demanded that Luther be brought to Rome to be tried.

Q. 37. Did Luther go to Rome?

A. No, Luther did not go to Rome. The Emperor, Charles V, thought it prudent to disregard the Pope, and instead cited Luther to appear before the Diet at Worms.

Q. 38. When did Luther answer before the Diet?

A. Luther answered before the Diet on April 17th and 18th, 1521.

Q. 39. Who was Luther's main opponent in trying to have him condemned at the Diet?

A. Luther's main opponent at the Diet was an Italian legate named Jerome Aleander.

Q. 40. What two questions were put to Luther at the Diet?

A. The two questions that were put to Luther at the Diet were: did he acknowledge that the books before him (about twenty-five in number) were his, and would he recant them.

Q. 41. What was Luther's answer?

A. Luther acknowledged the authorship of his books, but asked for more time to consider the question of recantation.

Q. 42. Was Luther granted more time?

A. Yes, Luther was granted one day.

Q. 43. Did Luther recant of his writings the next day?

A. No, after briefly explaining his books, Luther refused to recant them, and warned the Emperor not to begin his reign by condemning the Word of God.

Q. 44. What was Luther's memorable response to the question of recantation?

A. Luther's memorable response to the question of recantation was: *"It is impossible for me to recant unless I am proved to be in the wrong by the testimony of Scripture or by evident reasoning; I cannot trust either the decisions of Councils or of Popes, for it is plain that they have not only erred, but have contradicted each other. My conscience is bound to the Word of God, and it is neither safe nor honest to act against one's conscience. Here I stand, I can do no other. God help me! Amen."*

Q. 45. What was the Roman Catholic Churches decision that was rendered at the Diet of Worms?

A. The Roman Catholic Churches decision rendered at the Diet of Worms was that Luther's books were to be burned and forbidden to be printed and sold, he and his followers were not to be given sanctuary, and the magistrates were to seize and deliver him to Rome.

Q. 46. Were these decisions followed?

A. These decisions were not followed by the greater part of Germany.

Q. 47. Where was Luther taken by secret while on his way home from the Diet?

A. Luther was taken away by secret to the Wartburg castle.

Q. 48. Why was Luther taken there in secret?

A. Luther was taken there in secret to save his life.

Q. 49. Who arranged this action?

A. The Elector, Frederick "the wise" arranged this action.

Q. 50. How long was Luther at the Wartburg for?

A. Luther was at the Wartburg for nearly eleven months.

Q. 51. What did Luther do while at the Wartburg?

A. While at the Wartburg Luther translated the New Testament into German, and wrote many books, letters, and tracts on various theological subjects.

Q. 52. What was the significance in Luther translating the New Testament?

A. The significance of Luther translating the New Testament was that the Bible became the people's book in church, school, and home. It was now open for all to read in the common language of the people which brought the Gospel to their hearts and minds.

Q. 53. Did Luther translate the entire Bible?

A. Yes, Luther's first translation of the entire Bible was finished in 1534.

Q. 54. What effect did Luther's German translation of the Bible have on the people?

A. The effect that Luther's German translation of the Bible had on the people was that it became the most powerful help to the Reformation. Religious revival broke out as the people could now read the Gospel for themselves, resulting in the edification of the saints. The common man could now see for himself, from the Scriptures, Christian doctrine, with which he could now dispute with priests, monks, and doctors of divinity.

Q. 55. What was happening in Wittenburg while Luther was confined at the Wartburg?

A. While Luther was confined at the Wartburg, Andreas Carlstadt, fellow professor at Wittenburg, along with some men called the Zwickau Prophets, began to turn the Reformation into a revolution.

Q. 56. How were they turning the Reformation into a revolution?

A. They were turning the Reformation into a revolution by instituting many radical changes, inciting the people to destroy supposed idols, claiming to have direct revelations from God, and disparaging the Word of God and regular ministry of the Church.

Q. 57. How did Luther restore order at Wittenburg?

A. Luther restored order at Wittenburg by preaching eight sermons against the abuses and revolutionary tendencies of Carlstadt and the others. Luther also restored, for a time, some of the old religious forms which were removed, and began to bring in the needed reforms gradually.

Q. 58. Shortly after this restoration of order at Wittenburg, what two individuals did Luther have personal controversies with?

A. Shortly after the restoration of order at Wittenburg Luther had personal controversies with King Henry VIII of England, and Erasmus of Rotterdam.

Q. 59. What were the disputes with King Henry VIII and Erasmus of Rotterdam about?

A. The dispute with King Henry VIII concerned the sacraments; the dispute with Erasmus of Rotterdam concerned predestination and free will.

Q. 60. Who was Erasmus of Rotterdam?

A. Erasmus of Rotterdam was the most renowned scholastic theologian of his time. Erasmus had issues with Rome and was sympathetic to some of the ideals of the Reformation, but did not wish to see the Church divide over these issues.

Q. 61. Despite Erasmus' refusal to support the Reformation, how was he of essential help to it?

A. Erasmus was of essential help to the Reformation by his Greek New Testament which became the basis of the 'Received Text', which the Reformers used to translate the New Testament into the common language of the people.

Q. 62. What book did Erasmus write which launched the debate between him and Luther?

A. Erasmus wrote the 'Freedom of the Will', in which he taught that man was not totally corrupted from the fall, and that freedom of choice was an indispensable condition of moral responsibility, which launched the debate between him and Luther.

Q. 63. What was Luther's response to Erasmus' book 'The Freedom of the Will'?

A. Luther's response to Erasmus' book 'The Freedom of the Will' was his book 'The Bondage of the Will', in which Luther taught that man was totally corrupted by the fall and cannot will any spiritual good.

Q. 64. What war broke out in Germany in 1523 as people misunderstood spiritual freedom for license to sin?

A. The war which broke out in 1523 was 'The Peasants War'.

Q. 65. Why were the peasants grieved?

A. The peasants were grieved because they were virtually slaves to the wealthy with little relief from taxation and servitude.

Q. 66. What was Luther's opinion of the peasants grievances?

A. Luther's opinion of the peasants grievances was that, at first, he sympathized with them, but then turned against them when they openly rebelled.

Q. 67. Why was Luther adamantly against rebellion?

A. Luther was adamantly against rebellion because he believed, according to Romans 13:1, that Christians are to be subject to the authorities which God has set up, and that rebellion is one of the worst forms of disobedience.

Q. 68. Did the rebellion of the peasants succeed?

A. No, the peasants rebellion did not succeed. With the weighty support of Luther the princes put down the rebellion by force, killing around 100,000 peasants.

Q. 69. What was the result of The Peasants War?

A. The result of The Peasants War was that many of the peasants in south Germany went back to the Roman Catholic Church, embittered by the support Luther gave to the nobles, but it ultimately did not stop the progress of the Reformation.

Q. 70. When, and to whom, was Martin Luther married?

A. Martin Luther was married in 1525 to Catherine Von Bora, an ex-nun.

Q. 71. How did Luther justify the breaking of his monastic vow of celibacy?

A. Luther justified the breaking of his vow because he, *"...wished to please his father, to tease the Pope, and to vex the Devil." He "...held that God has created man for marriage, and that those who oppose it must either be ashamed of their manhood, or pretend to be wiser than God."* (Schaff, History of the Christian Church, Vol. 7, p. 455)

Q. 72. How many children did Luther and Catherine have?

A. Luther and Catherine had six children.

Q. 73. How was Luther's marriage significant to the Reformation?

A. Luther's marriage was significant to the Reformation because, though other priests already married, Luther's marriage set a precedent for Scripturally approved clerical marriage.

Q. 74. What was the next gathering of the princes to discuss the religious questions?

A. The next gathering of the princes to discuss the religious questions was the Diet of Nuremberg, which was held between 1522-1524.

Q. 75. What was decided at the Diet of Nuremberg?

A. The decision at the Diet of Nuremberg was to execute the decisions made at the Diet of Worms, but with the clause, "as far as possible."

Q. 76. What was the Diet named which was held in 1526?

A. The name of the Diet which was held in 1526 was 'The first Diet of Speier'.

Q. 77. What was decided at the first Diet of Speier?

A. The decisions which were made at the first Diet of Speier were that a general council should be convened for the settlement of the church question, and it was concluded that "every State shall so live, rule, and believe as it may hope and trust to answer before God and his imperial Majesty."

Q. 78. What was significant about the first Diet of Speier?

A. The significance of the first Diet of Speier was that it allowed the princes who were for the Reformation to strengthen it in their territories.

Q. 79. What was the name of the Diet which was held in 1529?

A. The name of the Diet which was held in 1529 was 'The second Diet of Speier'.

Q. 80. What was significant about the second Diet of Speier?

A. The significance of the second Diet of Speier was the order that no change of religion should be made until a council be held the following year, and that Lutherans should not be able to worship in Catholic territories but that toleration should be shown to Catholics in Lutheran territories.

Q. 81. What was the reaction of the Lutherans at the second Diet of Speier to this decree?

A. The reaction of the Lutherans at the second Diet of Spier to this decree was that they entered a formal Protest, which is where we get the name 'Protestant' from.

Q. 82. What was the name of the Diet which was held in 1530?

A. The name of the Diet which was held in 1530 was 'The Diet of Augsburg'.

Q. 83. What did the Emperor, Charles V, ask of the Lutherans when he summoned them to the Diet of Augsburg?

A. The emperor, Charles V, asked the Lutherans at the Diet of Augsburg to put forth their beliefs and point out where they differed from the Catholics.

Q. 84. What document did the Lutherans present at the Diet of Augsburg which expressed their beliefs?

A. The Lutherans wrote what is known as 'The Augsburg Confession' to express their beliefs at the Diet of Augsburg.

Q. 85. Who was the main author of 'The Augsburg Confession'?

A. 'The main author of 'The Augsburg Confession' was Philip Melanchthon, Luther's friend and fellow professor at Wittenburg.

Q. 86. What part did Melanchthon play in the Reformation?

A. The part that Melanchthon played in the Reformation was that he shaped much of the theology of the German Reformation, being referred to as "The teacher of Germany" because of his scholarly understanding of the Bible and his knowledge of Greek.

Q. 87. What was one of Melanchthon's great contributions to the Reformation?

A. One of Melanchthon's great contributions to the Reformation was his book 'Theological Common-Places' (or Loci Theologici) which became the first Protestant system of theology.

Q. 88. What major difference in theology existed between Luther and Melanchthon?

A. The major difference in theology between Luther and Melanchthon was that Melanchthon denied the absolute bondage of the human will in spiritual things, and held, rather, to a co-operation of the divine and human will in the work of conversion.

Q. 89. Did these differences hinder Melanchthon's fellowship and co-operation with Luther in the work of the Reformation?

A. No, these differences did not hinder Luther's and Melanchthon's co-operation and fellowship in the work of the Reformation. Luther held the highest regard for his friend and colleague.

Q. 90. What was the purpose of the Diet of Augsburg?

A. The purpose of the Diet of Augsburg was to settle the religious question and prepare for war against the Turks.

Q. 91. Did Luther attend the Diet of Augsburg?

A. No, Luther did not attend the Diet of Augsburg. It was not safe for him to do so because he was still under the ban from the Diet of Worms and would receive no protection outside of the Protestant states.

Q. 92. What, of significance, happened at the Diet of Augsburg?

A. Significantly, at the Diet of Augsburg, the Lutherans insisted on settling the church question, and pressed the emperor for the opportunity to read their confession publicly—this request being granted.

Q. 93. Did the reading of The Augsburg Confession bring the desired unity that both the Protestants and Catholics were looking for as they contemplated a war with the Turks?

A. No, the reading of The Augsburg Confession did not bring about the desired unity of both the Protestants and Catholics. It further widened the gap because there were certain evangelical articles which the Roman Catholics could not accept.

Q. 94. What was the end result of the Diet of Augsburg and The Augsburg Confession?

A. The end result of the Diet of Augsburg and the Augsburg confession was that each party, Protestant and Roman Catholic, went their own way and continued warring in word and action until 1555 when the "Peace of Augsburg" was signed, finally securing the legal right within Germany for Lutherans to worship.

Q 95. When did Martin Luther die and go home to be with the Lord?

A. Martin Luther went home to be with the Lord on February 18, 1546.